Feed It to the River

Feed It to the River

poems
Terhi K. Cherry

MOON
TIDE PRESS

~ 2022 ~

Feed It to the River
© Copyright 2022 Terhi K. Cherry

Editor-in-chief
Eric Morago

Editor Emeritus
Michael Miller

Marketing Specialist
Ellen Webre

Proofreader
LeAnne Hunt
Front cover art
Terhi K. Cherry

Author photo
Kenneth Wesley

Book design
Michael Wada

Moon Tide logo design
Abraham Gomez

Feed It to the River
is published by Moon Tide Press

Moon Tide Press
6709 Washington Ave. #9297
Whittier, CA 90608
www.moontidepress.com

FIRST EDITION

Printed in the United States of America

ISBN #978-1-957799-05-6

For Ken and Paloma

Contents

It Was Meant to Go Like This

When the head pops
out of my body, a spring fruit
crisp to bite, tiny fingers
curled over those eyes, the seeds
of an African star apple
fallen on top of me, latched
onto the sap of Nordic
winter, bile and debris
peeling away; we were tart
cherries jointed from a stem,
soon to be plucked.

When Are You Having Children?

I heard NASA found water on the moon's
sunlit side. I thought it was barren,
like Becky's cousin, an addict, who conceived
with her meth-cooking boyfriend.

Sarah's younger sister lives on soda
and chicken, expecting her second child.
I'm having a hard time believing
I should give up my cup of coffee.

Every morning I stumble, eyes half shut,
pee in a cup. Line up dollar store sticks
like suspects, month after a month,
a blank stare.

Because Venus can't support life in thick
atmospheres, I cut carbs. Because the dress
left hanging on the changing room door
belongs to a woman

whose children all died. The front porch
shrouded in wisteria, choking out anything living.
Like the lining of a womb grows into
wrong places, no mother

should bury her children. This is no
baby dance: Rachel pressures her depressed
boyfriend because the app screams
ovulation. Dana meets a donor

in a Starbucks restroom, a needleless syringe
in her handbag. Nitrogen tanks
mean empty bank accounts because
the insurance won't cover.

When Hannah walked from Harlem
to the Hudson River, she swore by exercise.
Saw seven pregnant ladies. The clinic
called: None of her eggs had fertilized.

She could try another round, jab another
needle, be a gut-hooked fish
thrown back in the sea. Or she could
break some windows.

She too had tried Mucinex, Robitussin,
grapefruit juice. Bit into pineapple
core. Hung upside down, pillows under
her hips, thinking she can't methylate.

She breathes four-seven-eight, slips on a dress,
hides unruly ovaries, sits by the door
in a baby-shower crowd, choking
on the name choices, the nursery décor.

A woman taps my hand, wants to know
when I am having children.
I want to tell her, a witch in Kalamazoo
hand poured me a candle,

I smeared it with what came out of me,
burned it for three days, found a dead moth
in the cutlery drawer, a pigeon's egg
near my door.

My mother just dangled her legs
out the window, and my father
asked for a smoke. In the next picture,
my brother was born.

I wish the moon would break its water,
bring the rain, drench me.

The Night I Sleep in the Nursery

I hear the yellow walls whispering.
My friend's baby has not arrived
alive. I place my guest towel
on the edge of that baby's crib,
see a white orb floating
in the room. I press my face
into a pillow, try to unsee
a howling woman thrust
a sleeping child onto paper sheets,
sink in the scent of lavender
and grief; my own grief
left by the door like an umbrella
wet from the rain. The body remembers:
I saved eggs like diamonds,
baked stars with apricots & sugar
dusted my man's lips.
I pictured us on a green lawn.
Nothing would stick;
the ovary ripened, only some days
the soil bears. Sometimes the egg
speaks: does not approve.
I do not compare
how lightning strikes from the sky's throat,
how a woman jolts from the shock of death,
how I scrubbed my blood off marble tiles,
convulsing, as if a spirit hatched out
of my open jaw. I do not say,
I saw the rocking chair moving
from nobody's weight.
Only the chair, rocking. Arms empty,
its lap wide open,
like a woman's biggest wound.

On the Other Side of Hope

was a circumstance, malleable like clay in the hands of a sculptor, the shape of a man and a house, the faded date on an egg carton. Hope, like the men you dated, like dive bars and hiking trails, like your cousins' children; how all of you were marigolds, the late season colors in bloom. Hope, a lover, a green backyard, the lies that fell like birds against your window and broke the glass. You wiped your face from a romance, walked to the edge of forty, alone, as if it were a cliff.

Perhaps the Life I'll Never Have

tucked inside a sleeping bag dreaming under the Milky Way wiped
out from campfire marshmallows heading northwest in the morning
waking up after rain in Reno searching for worms & ladybugs soon
balancing my baby on two wheels as she pedals if only yesterday I
changed her Pampers wiped banana off her face now she's laughing
jumping into a pool in Florida her front teeth have fallen those baby
vomit stains never faded from my shirt I'm playing tooth fairy spinning
school runs sticking drawings on the wall packing lunches my head
is turning to butter & crackers gushing at her grades how she'll be a
cheerleader & a quarterback how she paints like Tamara de Lempica
hands at the wheel of a green Bugatti becomes a math buff grabs a
scholarship chemistry or medicine endless arguments how her dress
hangs how a hickey blooms like a garden pansy how her red lips scream
MAC Ruby Woo stolen from Sally's she slams the door in my face like
a bitch slap & the night I find a gun tucked under her mattress beneath
the fairy lights where her head falls on a pillow she takes my car keys
& drives taillights fading like the stars

My Pear-Shaped Secret

Submerged in the abdomen,
between the bladder and the rectum,
sunken to the bottom of the sea,
the long axis bent forward; perhaps tipped
backwards; how would I know
if it was heart-shaped & kitsch;
if the wall of muscle collapsed, the center
split into neighboring apartments;
if it were a fun house
where a baby hangs upside down,
pushes out bottom first;
if it felt how Shulie Firestone put it,
like shitting a pumpkin?

When the Speculum Opens, I Remember

my head against her belly's soft aching,
an echo where her womb had been; and I,
once a baby, now the sound of her pain,
I can no longer have children. My five-year-old
ears are open, but mama never tells me why.
I imagine her missing parts, like the engine stolen
from a car abandoned, her *uterus* like a foreign
language, the empty space in the heart
of a cellar where I held my belly like a secret;
mama said, *when the blood comes,*
comes the babies, then disappeared,
as if a harp seal leaving her pup, falling prey
to wolves. I hid among the shrubs, twisted
and pig-tailed, flushing down sanitary
pads because mama never told me
it clogged the pipes. How else to dispose
the red flesh of berries smashed
open like a wound?

When Your Aging Mother Reveals Her Endometriosis in Passing

You never thought to pull up
the roots & look what you carried
from your mother
because all the flowers she planted
bloomed, & you watched
as she arranged perennials in soil,
gently untangling the knots, always,
such knowledge in her hands;
you grew up believing
little girls are made of geranium,
chrysanthemum & alstroemeria,
& when you tried to grow them,
spreading the root balls in the hole
in the ground, you watched
as they died in the sun,
each flower dropped their necks;
you never thought of lichen
on dead wood & tombstones,
wrapping around your wombs,
how your mother hushed up
those patterns on rocks
& boulders; how she looked,
doubled over in pain;
never thought it climbs up so silent,
that crusty growth on red cedar tree;
the only clue, your flowers,
hosta leaves turning yellow,
until she drops
the name of your beast.

Blink and You'll Miss It

the bright lights of Wendy's pop like yellow confetti we are hovering like ghosts at the hospital parking lot under the dark canvas of the sky in these unprecedented times in these freezing nights I am bleeding somebody please take my details my name is fourth miscarriage this week they say it must be in the air they say just take a seat they say we'll bring you a blanket don't be embarrassed minutes turn to hours the blanket never comes but there's a neon sign like a promise tonight people carry on scarfing fries out of paper bags we will jolt from this nightmare if we get up and scream I am next now I hop up on the table now the nurse taps my vein says your baby will be fine I must be dreaming they see nothing on the sonogram at five weeks I see nothing on her face like in a drive thru I am just passing through I am a stranger in the night I am tissue and bone she keeps staring at the screen if she blinks she will miss it

Underserved

No matter how you slice it,
score the skin with a paring knife,
you come apart, finding yourself
out of pocket, pregnant
and guilty, the phone numbers
listed are not ringing, the case worker
is never calling, unmedicated
you need to ask some questions,
entitled to the care you are seeking,
home births and breast pumps,
you may not have a choice
about caesarean, episiotomy,
a complaint sticks in your throat,
because of the language you spoke,
the insurance status, you are left
peeled on the table, hit with
the back of a spoon so that your
seeds fall out.

Feed It to the River

Nature knows the ending.
Somewhere, a river flows into the ground,
dries, never reaches the sea. Things stop
without a wonder. Salt depletes
the soil, heavy branches bend down,
the river claims a tree. Here,
it's like someone salted the earth to curse the land
so that I could never grow crops,
carry to term the buds that swell
and bloom. When a tree must sacrifice
the fruit unable to survive, nature coaxes
an answer: rodents eat what is fallen.
Just a seed, smaller than a segment of an orange,
will be passed from my body,
an empty sac I can flush without looking.
My first baby, washed out
like spores on the leaves, blotted out
on the stoic face of the tech who hurried me
from the changing room onto the table.
Carrying what had blighted, I chose the river.
Knowing, when the rain falls,
it runs the surface of the land like the first gush of blood,
opens its mouth to the sea as if singing,
it was nothing you did. There,
it may pour into my hands, my grain of rice,
crimson and shiny.
Blanketed by bay laurel trees,
a great blue heron atop a floating bed of kelp,
there, in the abundant light, I'll feed it
to the river.

The Silver Willow Weeps

and holds me, as I climb myself to its arms.
Soon my body is a wooden barrel,
the foliage falls in burnt orange;
maybe I could be happy
growing tomatoes on a vine,
seeing California chilis ripen to a deep red,
jazz radio blurring the noise of the US 101.
I'd like Encino, I said,
feeling young in unfiltered sunlight.
I wanted to land
in the embrace of pine trees and snow,
wake up to the coffee brewing
while my mother, still in her nightgown,
pours oats into a pan.
I could listen to the decades' old radio,
watching, as my mother throws salt in the porridge,
not remembering, she had already salted it.
I once believed
I would never carry an older woman's body,
never notice my hands' furrowed bark.
The willow wept
over the debris of dead babies,
where the life I wanted, shed.

Troubleshooting Loss

Your baby didn't die because of raw fish,
soft cheese, deli meat, or sex,

not because of exercise, the grocery bags,
or Tylenol,

not because of one bad choice, an argument,
the side you slept on,

not because of pinot noir before
you knew.

A scientist vows, one in four ends,
it doesn't mean it wasn't written:

the hue of the skin,
how the cheekbones would rise,

if hair locks would flock
and tangle.

Someone was taking root,
trying real hard to divide

into a cluster of diamonds,
into liver and lungs, to burrow into you

like you were a rock crevice
and the shoots of a hawthorn unreachable.

Watching Boys Skate,

long hair flowing under knitted
hats; jumping on their boards
like big cats, wild dogs;
falling on their backs, brazen;
springing back like antelopes,
as if nothing could hurt them.
Shaded from the glare of the sun,
I worry, would they fight a jackal
with their blunt claws?
Hand over my mouth, I stand
like a mother grieving.

When Cleopatra Lost Her Kingdom, She Ate a Fig

after Kornél Mundruczó and Kata Wéber's film, *Pieces of a Woman*

She doesn't fight, drives
her man to the harbor,

the passenger door shuts
like the last word.

At home, a ripe fig forgotten
in the fruit bowl,

one that Eve had plucked
instead of an apple,

the bud opening a teardrop,
the size of her thumb.

She thinks of the flesh,
how tender the skin

soaked in water,
how sweet the last bite;

the baby descending
in the canal

of her body like
to a creek,

the unmistakable urge
to push,

the blue velvet skin
turning to violet.

Sees it clearly now,
like the day staring

behind the open blinds,
how he drinks in a cheap room,

slips a fifty
into a stranger's bra,

pulls that girl
into his saddened lap.

Recalls the eyes
that hardly opened,

hands cupping the face
in the bath.

Is this acceptance —

he against a stranger's ribs,
she alone with a fig?

And what it would be like
to knock the bowl over,

squash the fig gently
under her foot,

release the sweet flesh
from its purple skin?

How to Save a Meringue

Giving progesterone to women with early
pregnancy bleeding and a history of miscarriage
could save 8,450 pregnancies each year.

— Research from The University of Birmingham and Tommy's, 2020

If you crack the shell gently,
leaving two halves in your hand,
carefully passing the egg from one half
to the other, back and forth,
like this limbo you are in; the whites
spilling out into the bowl
beneath your hands, leaving behind
the yolk, like a question;
and if you beat the whites to soft peaks,
the foam will harden like the fact,
the night you presented yourself
at the ER, the doctor didn't test your
progesterone; and if sugar
is not added slowly, the network
of protein that makes a meringue possible,
collapses like your lining, unable to thicken
and hold the embryo; and you'd think,
how a baker knows to stabilize a meringue
with something acidic—cream of tartar,
a splash of lemon—the doctor
would have done all in her power
when you told her, and told her again,
you were bleeding.

There Will Be a Day When You Meet Yourself at the River's Edge,

in a deep pocket of mountains,
agave sprouting along the sandy ridges;
carrying a box, wrapped in a cloth,
the ashes of a picture of how you dreamt your child,
a confession, how you need to let this pass;
watching crows catch each other in flight,
you wish to float like a body
sent out into the ocean, relinquish control.

Take the blade of a trowel to the earth,
scoop a mouth that swallows your dream whole,
think of the hands of a man
who throws bodies into the Yamuna,
into the black waters of Delhi, while here,
boys paddle the river in rental kayaks;
and you, kneeling on the sloping bank,
burying the dream of mothering,
sinking it into the throat of this world,
giving it back to the gods.

I Named You After Cherry Café

the greens and blues in my mother's voice

— Toni Morrison

because my father told me to smile lips closed & teeth retracted or
else the cows on pasture would die I sweated in a uniform popped
painkillers in the poultry plant tendons burnt finger broken & I named
you after the café by the gas station where I baked cinnamon buns for
truck drivers it was the one thing I succeeded in & when the police
stopped me I smiled lips pursed like a good Karelian evacuee & the
infection leached from a communal sauna & your father hurled a moldy
loaf of bread down the basement stairs I wanted better for you they
displaced us like herds in trains across the country & the kids in the
new school laughed at my language & no one helped with a bucket
I spilled my appendix on the floor scrubbed it on my knees until the
teacher showed mercy sent me home on a kick sledge across the field
of snow I stepped out of a boxcar an apple in my pocket saw the roofs
of our homes blow up to gaping mouths but we were called invaders
like the years of migraines a tumor crouched inside my cheek my
mouth a mine of mercury each tooth a darkened tomb but you were
beautiful everyone turned as you strolled in the white winter coat that
had cost me too much & when my pelvis inflamed like another town
was on fire I never told you they scooped out my womb how all of my
life I've been mourning hiding myself in the cattle car growing like
lesions in places I don't belong

As I Descend, My Mother Calls a Taxi

Like a ball of light I fall, all energy,
no head, arms, or legs; no blood or a body,
I float like an idea, hydrogen and helium,
rolling through the atmosphere
into a cell, from the wall of an ovary
into a sac, like a pearl into my mother's
pocket, where I sculpt
carbon, nitrogen, oxygen,
two eyes into the sockets of bone,
membranes into matter; I sleep for seasons
like a god, phosphorus in the vastness
of time, forgetting how the stars
ejected me, that I was older than the sun;
until the mid-March rain wakes me
tapping on the apartment window,
my mother's voice muffled on the telephone;
I am opening and softening,
stretching and burning, turning into a rush
of water, descending, becoming
my mother's breath in the backseat of a taxi,
moving through the passage of cervix,
until the crown of my head glows in red streaks,
and consciousness breathes upon me;
I am gasping, as if gravity sucked me
from the space dust onto the table,
looking at the tiny hands I had created,
the atoms of my skin vibrating still,
until my eyes adjust to the light.

It Would Have Been September
after Lucille Clifton's *'the lost baby poem'*

you would have been born in a crowded
hospital, in the year of pandemic,
Pine-Sol, and no insurance

we would have shared a ride with a stranger,
waddled out of the sedan, dilated
over hot asphalt,

tried to surge with the waves,
the latex-gloved hands reeling you
out of the river

under the fluorescent lights, on this sloped
side of town, between a real estate development
and a public open space

would I have known how to call you,
would I have known how to hold
your precious life

putting a tiny hat on your head,
like a honeysuckle blossoming
in the yard

wailing carried you in,
through the retrofitted parking lot,
past the laundry room foaming at the pipes

aching to show you to sea,
and the hummingbird hovering outside
every day since I lost you,

watching me
from the small deciduous trees.

About the Author

Terhi K. Cherry's work appears in *SWWIM Every Day, TIMBER, Rogue Agent, Literary Mama, Cultural Weekly, Un(mother) Anthology* & film, and elsewhere. Her poem "Driving Through Death Valley" was nominated for the Pushcart Prize by *Cultural Daily,* and her debut chapbook *Feed It to the River* is available from Moon Tide Press in 2022. Terhi lives in Los Angeles and facilitates poetry for personal growth.

Acknowledgements

Thank you to the editors of the following publications where some of these poems and their earlier versions have first appeared:

Thimble Literary Magazine — "As I Descend, My Mother Calls a Taxi"
SWWIM Every Day — "Troubleshooting Loss"
Rogue Agent — "When Are You Having Children?"
Literary Mama — "The Night I Sleep in the Nursery"
Un(mother) Anthology — "Perhaps the Life I'll Never Have",
   "How to Save a Meringue" and "There Will Be a Day When You
      Meet Yourself at the River's Edge"
Un(mother) film — "When Your Aging Mother Reveals Her
Endometriosis in Passing" and "How to Save a Meringue"

My deepest gratitude to my incredible editor, Alexis Rhone Fancher. This chapbook would not exist without her critical eyes and her unwavering belief in my work.

Thank you to Jessica Boatright at Growing Poetry leading the Un(mother) project, providing me a creative space to process the grief of miscarriage. Many of the poems written for the project have ended up in this book.

I want to acknowledge the teachers, mentors, and friends in poetry who have encouraged and supported my writing in any capacity, especially Jack Grapes and the Los Angeles Poets & Writers Collective, Perie Longo, Elya Braden, and Alyesha Wise and Matthew 'Cuban' Hernandez at Spoken Literature Art Movement.

My sincere gratitude to Eric Morago for giving this book a home at Moon Tide Press.

The poem "When Are You Having Children?" has been shaped by real experiences of countless women around the world. The names used are fictional and any resemblance to actual persons is coincidental.

Thank you to anyone who has opened up about the grief of losing a pregnancy or a child.

Patrons

Moon Tide Press would like to thank the following people for their support in helping publish the finest poetry from the Southern California region. To sign up as a patron, visit www.moontidepress.com or send an email to publisher@moontidepress.com.

Anonymous
Robin Axworthy
Conner Brenner
Nicole Connolly
Bill Cushing
Susan Davis
Kristen Baum DeBeasi
Peggy Dobreer
Kate Gale
Dennis Gowans
Alexis Rhone Fancher
HanaLena Fennel
Half Off Books & Brad T. Cox
Donna Hilbert
Jim & Vicky Hoggatt
Michael Kramer
Ron Koertge & Bianca Richards
Gary Jacobelly
Ray & Christi Lacoste
Jeffery Lewis
Zachary & Tammy Locklin
Lincoln McElwee
David McIntire
José Enrique Medina
Michael Miller & Rachanee Srisavasdi
Michelle & Robert Miller
Ronny & Richard Morago
Terri Niccum
Andrew November
Jeremy Ra
Luke & Mia Salazar
Jennifer Smith
Roger Sponder
Andrew Turner
Rex Wilder
Mariano Zaro
Wes Bryan Zwick

Also Available from Moon Tide Press

A Likely Story, Robbi Nester (2014)
Embers on the Stairs, Ruth Bavetta (2014)
The Green of Sunset, John Brantingham (2013)
The Savagery of Bone, Timothy Matthew Perez (2013)
The Silence of Doorways, Sharon Venezio (2013)
Cosmos: An Anthology of Southern California Poetry (2012)
Straws and Shadows, Irena Praitis (2012)
In the Lake of Your Bones, Peggy Dobreer (2012)
I Was Building Up to Something, Susan Davis (2011)
Hopeless Cases, Michael Kramer (2011)
One World, Gail Newman (2011)
What We Ache For, Eric Morago (2010)
Now and Then, Lee Mallory (2009)
Pop Art: An Anthology of Southern California Poetry (2009)
In the Heaven of Never Before, Carine Topal (2008)
A Wild Region, Kate Buckley (2008)
Carving in Bone: An Anthology of Orange County Poetry (2007)
Kindness from a Dark God, Ben Trigg (2007)
A Thin Strand of Lights, Ricki Mandeville (2006)
Sleepyhead Assassins, Mindy Nettifee (2006)
Tide Pools: An Anthology of Orange County Poetry (2006)
Lost American Nights: Lyrics & Poems, Michael Ubaldini (2006)

Made in the USA
Columbia, SC
05 February 2023

11234060R00024